Victim of Thoug

Seeing Through the Illusion of Anxiety

Jill Whalen

With a Foreword by Dr. Amy Johnson

ISBN: 9781521454206

Dedication

To my parents who must have done something right.

And to my husband, with whom I get to practice what I preach.

Table of Contents

Foreword

By Dr. Amy Johnson

What if—regardless of how anxious you feel—you are 100% healthy and well?

The first time I heard that question, I thought the person asking it was insane. "YOU certainly don't have complete mental health to propose such a crazy idea!" I thought.

I, perhaps like you, had struggled with a lifetime of anxiety and panic. I had a binge eating habit and was somewhere in the process of "kicking" several other destructive habits.

I was clearly *not* sitting in perfect mental health.

But then a funny thing happened. As I was feeling shocked and somewhat offended by the idea of me being 100% healthy and well, I also felt a wave of peace wash over me.

I found my mind was a little quieter; my heart a little more open. Something about the idea that we are fundamentally well by default, but are simply experiencing a steady stream of our own (sometimes anxious) thinking, felt right.

What if—regardless of the intensity of your anxiety (or depression, addiction, compulsions)—you are a healthy person simply experiencing anxious, depressed, and/or addictive thinking?

What if anxiety doesn't come from the world around you? What if it doesn't come from school or work, a change in schedule or lifestyle, or the people around you who seem to drive you nuts?

What if anxiety is your own moment-to-moment thinking masquerading as reality?

I realize these questions might sound a little crazy to you right now. They did for me when I first heard them. Yet the fact that you're reading this book means you're open to hearing something different. And as Jill mentions many times throughout *Victim of Thought*, having an open mind and seeing what feels right to you is the key to feeling better. Don't take my word or Jill's word for it. But as you read this book, hold these 'what ifs' loosely, and test them against your own feelings of truth.

I know the idea that you are healthy underneath your own steady stream of thinking is not what you were lead to believe. And it's certainly not what you may have heard from traditional psychology either.

But what if the premise of this book is true?

What if outside events really don't cause our stress and anxiety?

What if freedom from anxiety is a simple matter of—as the subtitle of this book suggests—seeing through the illusion of thought?

I've certainly found this to be true in my own life. And I've seen it to be true for the thousands of people I've served in my private practice as a psychologist and coach.

The new paradigm for psychology that *Victim of Thought* points to, is replacing old, outdated models. It is leading people worldwide to deep and lasting freedom, where many other methods have fallen short.

My clients come to me experiencing anxiety, habits, and addictions. The changes they experience after learning similar information to what Jill points you towards in this book, is incredible. It's no longer a question of them learning to *cope* with anxiety. They become truly free of it.

I am thrilled that Jill wrote this relatable, accessible book that will bring this new understanding of the human experience to many more people.

You are far more resilient, far closer to peace of mind and living your best life than you *think* you are (the italics are important there).

Hold that as a 'what if' as you read *Victim of Thought*, and see what you come to discover.

Amy Johnson, Ph.D.
Author of The Little Book of Big Change: The No-Willpower Approach to Breaking Any Habit and creator of The Little School of Big Change

Preface

A Few Words from the Buddha

Do not believe in anything simply because it is spoken and rumored by many.

Do not believe in anything simply because it is found written in your religious books.

Do not believe in anything merely on the authority of your teachers and elders.

Do not believe in traditions because they have been handed down for many generations.

But after observation and analysis, when you find that anything agrees with reason and is conducive to the good and benefit of one and all, then accept it and live up to it.

When I taught my SEO (search engine optimization/website marketing) training classes back in the mid-to-late 2000's, I read those words from the Buddha at the start of each class. Little did I know that 10 years later, I'd be using them again relating to a completely different subject.

It is my strong belief that everyone has to find a path that's right for them.

In the SEO industry, there were any number of "experts" one could listen to, or paths one could take to optimize a website and see results. I had personally developed my own common sense method. Not only did it get great results, but because of its simplicity, it resonated with my 25,000 newsletter subscribers, as well as with my clients.

Regardless of how confident I was of my method, I was adamant that nobody take my word for it. I knew it was important for people to try things out for themselves and see what resulted. I strongly believed that the only way for any of us to really learn was to gather our own evidence.

This was especially important with my teachings, because they were different from most others at the time. It was easy (and not unusual) for people to be skeptical of what I taught. Particularly when 99% of the consultants were saying one thing, and 'lil 'ole me was off in the corner saying nearly the opposite. Yet for those who would listen and hear the truth in my simple, practical words, success was generally a given.

Finally, after a good 17 years of swimming against the tide in the SEO industry, my form of common sense, back to basics, online marketing became the norm.

There are many parallels between what I used to teach and what I'm pointing people to now.

It may sound crazy that showing people where their anxiety comes from and teaching people about marketing their websites could be similar, but they are--at least in the way I talk about them. This is probably why I was drawn to the work of the late Sydney Banks in the first place. (Which provides the inspiration for what you will read in this book.) He boiled his common sense teachings down to the bare essentials--just like I always did. And because of that, his words rang true to me.

But Sydney Banks' teachings were also the opposite of what I and most everyone else in the world has been led to believe.

The simplicity of what he taught is what drew me to it; yet it's also what made it hard to swallow. At times, it even sounded counter-intuitive or too good to be true. At the very least, it went against everything I had previously learned. However, Truth is Truth. And that's what I heard from the very beginning--even if at first I didn't quite understand.

With that said, if something in this book rings the slightest bit true to you, I encourage you to give it a chance and explore it further. Even if you don't completely understand what you're reading at the time. The more evidence you find in your life that corroborates the truth of this information, the more it will make sense.

Once again I'm in the position where I don't want you to simply believe me or my words.

I implore you to always be searching for additional proof that supports the information in this book. That way you'll continue to know, without a doubt, how life really works--the opposite of how you think it does. It's only then, when you see the world anew through your own eyes, that the real fun begins!

Introduction

On May 1, 2013, after a few years of thinking about it, I decided to finally act on my desire to lose weight and live a healthier lifestyle. Little did I know the impact that one decision would have on my life! Six months later I came away with a body that was 25 pounds lighter, and a whole lot fitter. What I hadn't bargained for was the new personal identity that had apparently come along with my newly transformed body.

This unexpected change had me curious.

How could I go from proudly exclaiming I was "allergic to exercise and vegetables" my whole life, to abso-fricken-lutely LOVING them just six months later?

It was perplexing, for sure. But as I dissected what had happened, it became clear that personal identity wasn't as fixed as I thought. I had believed that hating vegetables was just part of who I was, yet obviously it wasn't.

This knowledge opened me up to new possibilities. If I could transform as much as I did from one simple decision to lose weight, what else might be possible to change?

I learned pretty quickly the next month when out of the blue, I decided to give up my lucrative SEO consulting business.

What made this decision seem a bit crazy to many (including me at times) was that SEO was not just a career path for me. It had been my life's passion for over 17 years. As a pioneer in that burgeoning industry, I took pride in knowing all the ins and outs, and had no lack of high-paying clients. Yet, I gave it all up for no particular (logical) reason. It simply *felt like* my work there was done, and it was the right thing for me to do at that time.

However, the aftermath of no longer being in the industry I knew and loved (and in which I was a prominent figure) for nearly two decades was another hit to my identity. If I was not an SEO consultant, and I also wasn't an out-of-shape, unhealthy eater--who the heck was I?

I decided to find out!

I started looking into psycho-spiritual stuff, and one day happened upon an online radio show hosted by a man named Michael Neill. He called himself a "Super Coach," which I thought was pretty hokey. But in listening to him speak with the show's callers--that's exactly what he was. Someone would call in with a problem, perhaps about their work, or their relationship or whatever. Michael would ask them a few questions and talk to them for maybe ten minutes; by the end, their problem was seemingly solved!

I found it fascinating and thought that Michael Neill was a true genius.

So I visited his website and signed up for his weekly newsletter. At the time, he was providing new subscribers with a link to a talk he had recently given. I immediately clicked the link and listened to it. My suspicions about his genius were confirmed. While I had no idea what he was talking about (I honestly thought I just wasn't smart enough) I could tell he was speaking the truth. And because my husband usually understood higher level things better than I did, I sent him the link to see what he thought. I hoped he might be able to dumb it down for me!

After my husband had listened to Michael's talk, I asked him what he thought was being conveyed. He said something to the effect of, "*It sounds like he's saying that it's our thoughts creating our feelings.*"

To which I responded, "I know! But what does that even mean?"

We left it at that, but both of us listened over and over to that one talk when we had a chance. Each time, I felt like I was getting it a little bit more. But, for the most part, I was still confused. At some point, I found and listened to another of Michael's talks. In this one, he was being introduced by a guy named George Pransky. During the intro, George mentioned something called "The Three Principles."

My heart sank.

All I could think was, "Michael Neill is in some sort of cult?"!

I was very confused. I really liked what Michael had to say, but I didn't want to keep exploring something kooky or cultish.

However, my next thought was, "Michael seems way too smart to be part of a cult."

So I cautiously went searching for more information on this whole Three Principles thing. (I'm pretty sure I went incognito on my Chrome browser so as not to be deemed part of a cult by Google!)

At first I found a website about a guy named Sydney Banks who, in my mind, appeared to be the "cult leader." The website was horribly out of date, without much information, and apparently Mr. Banks had passed away some years before. I then found a more up-to-date website with lots of free videos called, "ThreePrinciplesMovies.com." While there were a variety of presenters showcased there, I specifically searched for talks given by Michael Neill. (I was really stuck on this cult thing, and truly concerned about getting sucked into it somehow!)

Once I had exhausted all of Michael's talks, I decided (again cautiously) to watch some of the others. I chose to watch one put out by the creators of the website--a young English couple named Jenny and Rudi Kennard. It was a video recording of an introduction to The Three Principles workshop they had given.

I was pleasantly surprised!

I really loved their common sense way of talking. I could see the similarities to what I had heard Michael say, but there was something more down-to-earth in the way they spoke. They associated their teachings to real-world things such as how their relationship had improved. I especially liked listening to Jenny. I could totally relate to her stories about growing up painfully shy and anxious.

Once my mind was at ease that this Three Principles stuff *was not* a cult, I was better able to listen. Eventually, my paying attention paid off in other ways. I was gifted with some amazing insights that further impacted my personal identity and my life.

What I heard and learned from the teachings of Sydney Banks, Michael Neill, Jenny and Rudi Kennard and others in the Three Principles Community and beyond, has truly been a gift. My ongoing transformation has been nothing short of amazing--with the most significant changes having to do with anxiety.

Which is where this book comes in.

While there are many topics I could have written about such as having better relationships, addiction, personal identity, etc., those aspects of my life changed when my understanding of anxiety changed. My hope is that my story may inspire you, as well as provide a promise for more overall peace in your life as it has done for mine.

Before we begin, it's important to note that while my experience of anxiety may or may not be the same as yours, what I'm sharing here will still be helpful. You may believe that your level of anxiety must be worse than mine was for something so simple to have helped. But I assure you that what worked for me can, and has, helped alleviate all levels and forms of anxiousness in others. Whether you have long-lasting panic attacks every day, or you lived in a state of low-level anxiety off and on--there's *always* the potential for a complete shift in the way you feel.

All it takes is an insight into the true nature of life.

For the most part, I never let my anxiety stop me from participating in the world--it was simply a part of my life. If you asked me, I may not have even characterized myself as an "anxious person." It was only after I clearly saw a dramatic change in how I felt in any given moment, that I realized just how much anxiety I had been living with my entire life.

That said, there are tens of thousands of people (or more) who have lived with high levels of anxiety that have been set free upon insightfully understanding similar information to that in this book. Many of them have been diagnosed with crippling conditions such as post-traumatic stress disorder (PTSD) and others. (See the Resources Section in "Part 4" of this book to learn more.)

Whatever level of suffering you have is irrelevant.

I realize that's a bold statement. However, as long as you're open to the possibility that things can be different, there's the potential to feel better. This is why I encourage you to read this book with an open mind. It's also a good idea to try not to compare it with other psychological concepts you may have learned in the past. While you may see similarities, it's the differences that carry the promise of instant transformation.

There are four parts to this book:

Part One: Life With Anxiety - This is an autobiography of sorts that showcases some specific times in my life where I felt especially anxious. I've written it to show that I am just a regular human being who, for whatever reason, had a tendency to be anxious. I may have been born that way, things may have happened to me that scared me, or some combination of both. The reasons for my anxiety (or yours) are not important. My hope is that reading my story may invoke similar memories for you, which may now be seen from a new perspective.

Part Two: The Inside-Out Explanation - This gets into the nitty-gritty of what anxiety actually is, why we have it, how we cope with it, as well as why knowing the truth of where it comes from can have a freeing effect on us. This is the meat of the book in terms of learning a different way of seeing the world. It's also where I want you to seek your own evidence. My description of anxiety will likely be different than others you've heard before. Keep an open mind and try not to overthink my words. By doing so, you may gain some insights that relate to your own life. This is the key to unlocking anxiety's grip on you.

Part Three: Uncovering Our Inner Peace - Building upon the previous sections, this part provides you with ways to explore and deepen your newfound knowledge and insights. It's even more hopeful in that you'll learn about the presence of peace within you, which is accessible at any time. Plus, you'll learn how my relationship to my anxiety changed *automatically* after having some "aha moments" of my own.

Part Four: Where to Go From Here - This section is a small sampling of other authors, coaches, psychologists, websites, etc. where you can start to learn more about the inside-out understanding on which this book is based.

So, without further ado, let's get straight to the good stuff!

PART ONE:

LIFE WITH ANXIETY

Chapter 1: The Little Girl

Once upon a time, there was a little girl who had an older brother and a younger sister. Because her mom was concerned about "middle child syndrome" (which was the pop psychology of the day) she often told the little girl she was "not too big and not too small, but *just right!*"

She believed her mom and felt "just right" most of the time.

Except when she was full of fear.

Which happened quite a lot when she was around people she didn't know.

When out and about, she'd stick close to her mom and try not to look at all "the people." She hoped that if she wasn't looking at them they wouldn't notice her--or worse--try to talk to her. She really hated when they wanted to speak with her. It always seemed scary as she never knew what to say.

It wasn't just talking to strangers that scared her. If she was in a store and saw someone she knew, rather than going over and saying "Hi," she'd do whatever she could to hide from them. The last thing she wanted was for them to see her and then have to speak with them. The very thought of this tied her up in knots. It was always a relief when she managed to avoid them all together.

When she was 5 years old, the little girl went to Kindergarten. While she was nervous at first, she was happy to be able to go to school like her big brother. Her teacher was nice, which put her mind at ease. While she liked a lot of the kids in her class, there were a few who looked or acted "weird" to her. She found them a little scary, so she kept her distance and simply observed them from afar. For the most part, Kindergarten went smoothly.

First grade took a little getting used to. She had a new teacher and different kids in her class, but eventually the little girl settled in without too much trouble. However, one day towards the end of the school year, her teacher wasn't there. For some reason her entire class was moved to the cafeteria. Other classes were also spending the day there, and she found herself in among many new (scary) faces all around.

Amidst all the noise, clatter, chaos and confusion, she felt very alone.

Suddenly, her belly started to hurt--a lot. She'd never felt such stabbing stomach pains before, and she began to cry. Some kids noticed this and told the teacher on duty. The little girl was promptly escorted to the nurse's office.

There (and perhaps as soon as her mom arrived at school to take her home) the pain in her belly seemed to loosen its grip, and she started to feel better.

But the next morning when she was supposed to be getting ready for school, she felt that same sharp stabbing pain in her belly as the day before. Presuming she must have come down with something, her mom let her stay home. The little girl enjoyed the special treatment of getting to watch TV in her room, having tomato soup with Ritz Crackers (her favorite) for lunch, and spending time with her mom. She never thought much about the bellyache again throughout the day.

The next morning when it was time to go to school, however--OUCH! Her belly began to hurt again. Worried, her mom made an appointment to see the doctor. Her stomach was tied in knots during the ride to the doctors as she wondered what might be wrong with her. Did she have some terrible sickness? This thought came with another stabbing pain.

Once in the examining room, the doctor pushed and prodded her stomach and the surrounding area and declared that there didn't seem to be any physical issue. And, because she had no fever, she was okayed to go back to school the next day.

Next morning--more belly aching.

This time, however, because of her clean bill of health from the doctor, both of her parents told her she had to go to school. Upon hearing this news she thought her belly just might explode, and she started to cry. Nevertheless, she was forced to get dressed, placed in the car, driven to school and brought directly to her class. While her classroom and teacher were all back to normal with no "scary kids" around, her bellyache continued. So did her crying. Presumably, the teacher had been apprised of the situation and therefore paid no attention to the sad, hurting little girl in the back of the room.

This scenario repeated itself for days, but the school year soon came to a close for summer.

The little girl enjoyed her time off from school. She swam in her family's pool and played outside with her sister and the neighborhood kids. Her stomach problems seemed to have magically vanished with the end of first grade.

Come fall and the start of 2nd grade, the little girl once again had a bellyache on the first day of school (and a fitful night of sleep as well!). As young as she was, *even she* was noticing the connection to her stomach hurting and having to go to school. It was pretty obvious that her belly was fine all summer, but as soon as it was time for school it started hurting again.

So she did her best to ignore it.

Upon meeting her new teacher and seeing that she recognized most of the kids in her class, she soon forgot about her belly and just had fun. The rest of second grade, as well as most of her elementary school years, went off without any major problems. Her belly would still hurt at times when she got scared, but because she knew the connection to her nerves, she learned to live with it.

Chapter 2: Why Me?

Over time, the little girl became a bigger girl. She usually enjoyed school and learning and having fun with her friends and family.

Then 6th grade happened.

It started out uneventfully for the now teenage girl. While it had been stressful and an adjustment getting used to Middle School, having a locker, a schedule and multiple classes--she figured it out okay.

She had been somewhat "weirded out" by boys who looked like men (with beards and moustaches) roaming the halls, but after a while it didn't faze her much. She even adjusted to having to hold onto her books tightly so that the bigger (mean) kids couldn't knock them out of her arms "for fun" as they were prone to do in Middle School.

On one fateful day, however, she and another girl got called to the office at the end of classes. This was unusual as she was "a good girl" who kept quiet and generally didn't do anything wrong. Upon arriving at the office, she and the other student were given new class schedules. They were told to disregard their old ones and to start using the new schedules right away. There was no reason given to them for this change, and there didn't seem to be any choice in the matter.

So the next day, she had to find her classes and figure out her new schedule. As someone who was prone to getting lost, she felt very anxious about this. Prior to the schedule change, all her classes had been on the first floor. Her new schedule, however, had some classes upstairs. Just when she had finally felt familiar finding her way around the downstairs of the school, she now had to venture into new territory. "*Why me?*" she thought angrily.

Eventually she managed to navigate her way to her first new class, and showed the teacher her amended schedule. She was pointed to a seat in the back of the room and told to sit there.

As she surveyed her new surroundings, she didn't recognize any of the kids except for the other girl whose schedule had changed. They all looked really, really scary and mean. So she sat in her new seat in her new class, feeling very isolated, afraid and angry.

To herself, she again asked, "*Why me?*"

When class was over and she got up to leave, it seemed as if everyone was looking at her--almost as if they were right up in her face. She felt nervous and alone, and kept her head down so as not to see their scary faces. The old (now familiar) bellyache was back, but knowing that it was "just nerves" kept her from heading straight to the nurse's office--even though she desperately wanted to.

For the next few months she went to her new classes, but was angry about her situation. She didn't understand why she had to be with all these new (weird) kids while everyone else got to stay in the good classes with the nice kids. In her mind, it was wrong and unfair. "*Why me?*" seemed to be her new mantra. "*Why did all this bad stuff have to happen to me?*" was a constant thought in her head. She was confused by her situation and believed "they" didn't have the right to make her go through all this anguish for no reason at all.

With this line of thinking, she consciously or unconsciously decided she'd "*show them.*"

And with that, she simply gave up on school.

So it wasn't a huge surprise when report cards came out she got D's and F's in her new classes. This was quite a switch from her usual A's and B's with perhaps an occasional C. However, she hadn't thought through the consequences of her decision to give up. While her parents weren't sticklers about grades, the one thing they were adamant about was that you had to try your best.

Her report card was a clear indication that she was *not* trying her best.

While she had her reasons for giving up on her classes, the "unfairness of it all" wasn't something she could articulate or had ever talked about with her parents. And her attempt to not show her report card to them was quickly thwarted. It wasn't long before they heard from others that report cards were recently distributed, and asked to see hers.

Needless to say, the once good girl felt like a really bad girl and got into all kinds of trouble at home.

Chapter 3: Anxiety's Role

Of course, you've probably guessed that the little girl was me. The story is true in the sense that it's how I remember it through my adult eyes and current understanding of life.

It's clear to me now that I had a lot of anxiety running through me at various times in my life. I could be fine one minute and then something would happen which would throw me for a loop, and once again, I'd be under anxiety's spell.

For whatever reason (and it really doesn't matter why), new situations and especially new people scared me. As long as my routine went undisturbed, I was usually okay. But plunk me into unfamiliar territory and I completely fell apart and the old "*why me?*" sentiment would return.

While I wouldn't say that I had panic attacks (at least not the way I've heard others describe them), I had a sort of low level of anxiety buzzing around in the back of my brain and body throughout my life. It seemed that I never knew what uncertainty might be lurking around the corner, so I had to always be on alert.

My anxiety was especially acute in social situations where I didn't know others. One-on-one conversations felt especially painful. So I gravitated towards having one best friend (usually a chatty, outgoing girl) who I would cling to for dear life until they couldn't stand me anymore. A pattern that continued well into my adult years.

I also found alcohol at the young age of 14. At first it was just drinking in the woods with my neighborhood friends. But throughout high school, alcohol became a common crutch. It seemed to soothe my feelings of anxiety and made it easier to speak with others in social settings like parties and dances. I also tried smoking pot a few times, but that made me feel worse. I would get paranoid and think that everyone was pointing and whispering about me. I definitely did not need that!

In college I drank a fair amount, but it was socially acceptable and I never thought much about it--it was just what we did in college. I was also very close with my roommate who was outgoing and easy to be around. Once I started dating my future husband in my junior year, I began partying a lot less. I didn't realize it at the time, but I began to look to him to provide me with my good feelings, rather than alcohol or my best girlfriends.

We got married soon after I graduated college, and had our first child four years later. I was literally living out my dream of being married to my Prince Charming and being a mom at home with my children. As long as life went smoothly, I remained mostly happy.

Yet we all know how often that happens!

Without realizing it, anxiety was continuously playing in the background of my mind.

I had naturally developed all sorts of coping mechanisms to deal with it. My constant desire to feel good and find some sense of peace caused me to get immersed in things and people I liked, and avoid those I didn't. If I had to do stuff I didn't like, it never hurt to have a few drinks before, during and/or after.

But some things can't be avoided or "drunk away."

My greatest anxiety during that time was when any of my kids were sick. I would often find myself thinking the worst, even with minor illnesses. I remember one winter when my oldest daughter had a really bad cold that turned into asthma. I *literally* thought she was going to die before winter was over from not being able to breathe. I had many sleepless nights imagining this horrible scenario. (When I mentioned this to her recently she thought it was amusing. Apparently in her mind it was never a big deal!)

I was also anxious when it came to my own health. Doctors scared the crap out of me, and I had "white coat syndrome," which caused my blood pressure to skyrocket at appointments.

Yet through it all, I somehow managed my anxiety fairly well without realizing it. I was still quiet and shy on the outside, but most people would not have guessed I was anxious.

After all, I had done a really good job of finding ways to escape my bad feelings.

Chapter 4: Passion or Addiction?

While I managed to cope with my anxiety and keep it under control, unfortunately, my escape mechanisms were addictive in nature.

When my husband decided to go to law school in the early 1990's, he needed to have a laptop and modem (which was rare back then) to access a legal database. I was in heaven finally getting to have a computer in the house. I had fallen in love with them in my job after college at a now defunct company called Prime Computer.

When my husband wasn't using the laptop, I spent as much time as I could fiddling around with it and figuring out how to get online. Mind you, this was in the early 1990's, so the commercial internet was new. It was not readily apparent how to access and use it. Everything was done via text and typing not via images or mouse clicking. As a lifelong do-it-yourselfer, figuring it out was a dream come true for me.

When I was on the computer, I felt peaceful and happy.

Prior to getting the laptop, my obsession at the time had been parenting. Besides spending most of my days playing with my kids as a mom at home, I was constantly reading parenting literature. Once I had the computer and the internet, I was able to pair my two passions by creating an online parenting chat room and website. There were literally only two other parenting websites at the time, so mine became very popular.

It felt great to be able to do the things I loved most in life.

I spent hours in front of the computer when my girls were at school and my son was napping or playing quietly. Being on the computer, learning new things about working with websites, and chatting online about parenting--what could be better? As long as I got to do those things I was happy. But when something or someone took me away from all that-- not so much.

It felt like my peace of mind was being stripped from me.

In fact, at one point during this time our computer broke down. With my husband just out of law school, we had no money to get a new one and I was devastated. I had never been prone to depression, but losing that computer brought me close. My husband couldn't help but notice how horrible I felt. Thankfully we were just about to receive a tax refund, and he agreed that we could spend it on a new computer. *Just knowing that* seemed to lift my spirits big time. Once I heard the familiar "handshake" whistle of the modem connecting to the internet from our spiffy new computer, I was back to my old self. Phew!

Chapter 5: Finding My Voice

Eventually, my love of the internet and websites led to my career and business as a consultant and pioneer in what was the brand new website marketing field of SEO (search engine optimization).

I had managed to figure out for myself what search engines (pre-Google at that point) were looking for within websites in order to show them highly in their search results pages. Always wanting to share my knowledge with others, I began writing about it for free. Eventually people and businesses started to ask for my help and advice to market their websites, and my company, High Rankings, was born.

As someone who had trouble talking with new people in person, suddenly having a voice through my writing (and a strong one at that) and online work opened up a new world for me. I learned I had a natural talent for writing, as well as for explaining complicated topics in simple terms. This ability gave me a newfound confidence in communicating with others that I never had before.

Not only were people listening to what I had to say, they were praising my words!

Even with my new level of confidence, during the first few years of my business I wouldn't speak to clients by phone--all of my work was done online via email. While I could express myself brilliantly and beautifully through my writing, my anxiety kept me from actually talking to people.

As my business acumen grew, I was eventually able to talk about SEO as well as I wrote about it. It felt freeing to be knowledgeable about something and able to speak my mind, as opposed to sitting around listening to what everyone else had to say, as I had done for most of my life. And boy, did I have a lot to say!

How shocking it was when people were actually listening to me and seeing me as an authoritative expert in my field! Not only did I consult with many top companies, I also became a regular speaker at industry conferences around the world. While that may seem odd for someone with as much shyness and social anxiety as I had, for some reason I actually enjoyed public speaking. I got nervous, but as long as I was prepared and remembered that I was there to share my expertise, I was fine. In fact, it was exhilarating!

Harder was the social aspect of conferences.

I drank a lot of alcohol while there--the likes of which I hadn't seen since college. It helped that I was a speaker and well known in the industry. Attendees often recognized me and wanted to talk to me, which meant I rarely had to play any scary networking games. I also made quick friends with many of the other speakers who knew of me and had some respect for my work.

But unless I was talking about SEO (my passion/obsession at the time), my fear of unfamiliar faces and small talk would resurface. Thankfully, my old friend alcohol was freely available, and most of the others I hung around with were also imbibing in high quantities. (Perhaps they were as anxious as I was?)

When I'd come home from a conference it felt like I needed a good week of "detox." Both my alcohol-laden body and my overstimulated mind from being around and talking to so many people, needed a break. I literally just wanted to sit at my computer quietly for a few days and not have to speak with anyone--including my husband and children.

Chapter 6: The Birth of "New Jill"

As our kids got older, my husband and I had the freedom to go out and socialize more. While I would have been happy to stay at home, he is an extrovert who likes talking to and being around people. At first we'd go to a local bar on weekend afternoons to watch a few innings of Red Sox baseball. It was relaxing and a nice way to reconnect with each other. We'd usually have one or two beers, and then head home when the game was over.

Eventually we started hanging out at one particular neighborhood bar (think Cheers), and became friends with many of the "regulars." Over time, I found myself drinking more and more alcohol.

I drank for a number of reasons.

For one, we were hanging out at a bar and drinking is what you do there. But I also found that alcohol seemed to alleviate any problems or stresses that were weighing on my mind from work or my kids or some imagined health issue. The drinking also made it easier for me to chat with others at the bar.

During this period I was really enjoying my drinking. If someone told me they were going to take it away, I would not have been a happy camper. While I knew I could go for days without a drink, I wasn't quite sure how I'd be without it for a longer period of time. Yet I never thought of this as a problem, nor did I see any connection with it to my anxiety. In my mind, I was just having fun.

As menopause approached, between my hormones, my drinking and eating unhealthy bar food every night, I put on weight. I could no longer ignore the fact that I was--okay I'll say it--fat. It was amazing how many buttons I could burst through, mirrors I could turn away from, jiggles I could ignore and photos I could somehow believe the camera was adding ten (or twenty-five) pounds to.

As a small person growing up in a thin family, I had sworn I would never "go on a diet." I couldn't understand how friends through the years (as far back as high school) felt the need to diet. "*Just eat in moderation,*" I thought to myself, "*Dieting is dumb and for losers.*" When I was left at least five pounds heavier after each baby--and I had three of them in six years--it didn't bother me. I never actually weighed myself, but I wasn't necessarily displeased with my slightly curvier, rounder, more womanly figure that I maintained throughout my 30's and into my 40's.

I continued to eat what I wanted, when I wanted, and didn't think a whole lot about it. Although, come to think of it, much of my snacking back then was done when no one else was looking--which should have tipped me off at some point.

Once I reached my mid-to-late 40's, I realized I couldn't keep downing half a package of Peanut Butter M&M's or Ritz Bits while chatting with my online friends at midnight. So for the most part, I put a stop to that. I didn't keep stuff like potato chips or ice cream in the house anymore either. In fact, I only had black coffee for breakfast and what I thought was a smallish lunch and dinner. Yet, I was "growing out of" my clothes for some reason. (Damn that dryer!)

At the time I didn't realize that changing hormones can be a contributing factor to weight gain in women of a certain age. I also tried not to think about the drinks I was having every night, which had now grown from a few a week to a few a night. To even consider giving those up was out of the question. Social drinking had become a pleasurable routine. It seemed to provide me with some peace, and I was enjoying spending time with my husband. However, it wasn't just the extra calories from drinks I was taking in--eating out every night wasn't doing me any favors either.

As to what I was eating, while it wasn't large quantities, it certainly wasn't healthy. I had never met a vegetable that I liked. Honestly, I was afraid to try most of them. And even if I did like them, our local bar was severely lacking in the veggie department. (I'm pretty sure the most vitamins barflies get are from the limes in their drinks!)

While it seems I was able to eat unhealthily as a young woman, it had finally caught up with me.

I'm convinced that at this time in my life, my health was a ticking time bomb. I am just grateful that my inner wisdom kicked in before it detonated.

There was no one thing that finally broke the camel's back and got me to take action. It was more of a gradual realization that it was time for me to do something, and I was ready. The more I heard about others I knew who had lost weight, the more I was inspired to give it a shot. I had already been practicing yoga for a year and a half (although I still couldn't even do one push-up), and I was walking a bit more as well. So it wasn't too much of a stretch to finally decide to change my diet.

While I didn't call it "going on a diet" as that had such negative connotations for me, that's essentially what I did. Thank goodness for apps like MyFitnessPal and Fitbit. For an online tech junkie like me, they made it not seem so bad, and even a little bit fun.

According to my apps, for my height of 5'3" I could eat 1200 calories a day and lose about one pound a week, which seemed reasonable. At the time, I had no idea what 1200 calories of food even looked like. Plus, I had to figure in my two very strong alcoholic beverages a night, which I was guesstimating to be at least 300 calories. So I was down to 900 for actual food. Yikes!

Surprisingly, once I learned which foods had lots of calories but came in small amounts, e.g., butter and oil, simply removing them (or using very little) was an easy way to keep within my limits. Fried foods were definitely out. "Skinny" breads were in. Portions were controlled. When I learned that giant plates full of vegetables (or salads) had very few calories, they were in, even if I didn't enjoy them that much at the time. Shrimp--in! I often ate a big salad with Cajun shrimp for dinner at our bar along with my two strong drinks, and stayed within my calorie limit.

I started walking a lot more, and went to yoga class more often which enabled me to have a few extra calories to eat (or drink). However, it became clear that food choices were going to be more important than the exercise when it came to calories in and out.

And it was working!

I was losing a pound a week and sometimes even more.

Plus, I didn't feel like I was depriving myself. In fact, somewhere along the line, I started trying more healthy vegetables because they had fewer calories than other foods. I shocked myself when I realized I could not only eat a giant plate of asparagus for lunch at about 100 calories, but that I loved the way they tasted! Thank goodness too, because when I think about it now, I was eating so few calories I couldn't have been taking in an appropriate amount of nutrients. (Not that I was previously getting them.)

The cool thing is that once the weight started coming off, I found that I was able to do so much more in my yoga class. My appendages could bend in ways they previously couldn't, simply because there wasn't so much fat around them. And having less weight to push up meant that finally, finally, finally, I could actually *do* some push-ups!

Which of course all built onto itself.

Once I could do some push-ups, my upper body got even stronger. Then I could do *more* push-ups, and more of everything. The stronger and healthier my body became, the more energy I had and the more I craved healthy foods.

Plus, in a surprising twist, I naturally started drinking less alcohol.

At first it was to save the calories, but at some point, because I was feeling good about myself and less anxious, I wasn't as interested in drinking. In fact, I was starting to dislike hanging out at the bar. While I had a lot of friends there, being sober at a bar gets boring quickly. Plus, I felt bad taking up a seat and only having soda water, which sometimes made it more tempting to drink alcohol.

Within about seven months, I had reached my goal of losing twenty-five pounds.

For a few more months, I continued to count calories, but the more I learned about nutrition and health, the more I realized that this wasn't the best way to continue. Instead, I started eating even more vegetables, especially green ones, as well as lots of healthy fats and proteins, while limiting my grain intake.

Coincidentally (or not), soon after transforming my body was when I decided to further change my life by giving up my career and identity as an SEO consultant.

And New Jill Was Born!

As of this writing, four years from when I made my decision to lose weight and get healthy, I can take or leave the alcohol. My husband and I still like to hang out at our local bar, but I'm happy to have one drink or none at all. If I have more than one, it's generally over a very long period of time. And I haven't felt "buzzed," nor have I wanted to, in many years. At age 56, I'm in better shape than ever before in my life.

While my healthy way of eating and new lifestyle was certainly a catalyst for a lot of my personal transformation, the greatest change came from having some huge insights into my anxiety and my addictions.

Which brings me to the heart of this book and why I'm sharing my story with you.

PART TWO:

THE INSIDE-OUT EXPLANATION

Chapter 7: Understanding Anxiety

The changes in me caused me to see the world in a very different way. I started wondering how it was that I hated vegetables one day then loved them the next.

I became very curious about personal identity.

Which is how I stumbled upon Michael Neill's radio show and his inside-out understanding of life. This simple, yet profound understanding transformed my life even further.

It's an *understanding* in the sense that it's a different way of looking at the world. And it's *different* in the sense that while 100% true, it goes against everything most of us have been brought up to believe.

Quite simply, here's what I learned through my self-study and the insights that came out of it, which essentially switched off my lifetime of low-level anxiety:

While it appears that life is happening outside of us and TO us, in reality, our perception of life is created WITHIN us--via the Principle of Thought.

This is key because it illustrates a simple misunderstanding of the way most of us believe life works. When we assume life is happening *to us*, it takes away our feeling of control--which is darn scary. That belief alone creates a lot of anxiety, as we become victims of circumstance.

When we see for ourselves that *we* create our own experience of life--via our thoughts--we feel more secure. When we understand what's going on around us cannot *make us* feel a certain way, e.g., bad, scared, sad, mad, etc., it puts *us* back in the driver's seat.

For example, in my 7th grade experience of having a changed class schedule with new kids in a different part of the school building, it *looked to me* as if scary things were happening *to me*. But what about the other kid whose schedule had also changed? Did she experience the situation the same way I did? I honestly don't know, but I'm willing to bet that it was different for her.

There are an infinite number of ways anyone could have experienced the very same situation.

It's doubtful that everyone would have seen those new kids as scary-looking. Surely someone else may have found the whole thing to be a cool new adventure. Perhaps another may have been sick of their old schedule and happy to have a new one.

There are any number of feelings I could have had.

In other words, I, myself, created my own experience.

Don't get me wrong. This is not to say that I *made up* the situation. And it's not to place blame on myself for feeling the way I did. Obviously, there were certain facts involved. My schedule was changed. I had to go to a different part of the building for my classes. And there were definitely kids I didn't know there. But despite those facts, it's the way my particular mind processed and *thought about it*, that caused me to feel the way I did.

My unique personal experience of the event was based on everything I had learned and believed about myself and my life up to that point. In other words, the way my mind happened to *think* about those kinds of things.

If my life had been different, I would most certainly have had other thoughts, and therefore a completely different experience.

There's no getting around the fact that it was my thoughts, and not the circumstances, that caused me to feel the way I felt.

At this point, you may be looking for me to provide you with some scientific references that explain this inside-out nature of life. While I believe it is backed up by science, it's more important for you to witness the validity of it in your own mind. (This is one of those times mentioned in the Introduction, where I want you to seek out your own proof.)

Confused? Don't worry.

In the next chapter I'll go into more detail about the power of Thought, which will help clear things up for you.

Chapter 8: What is Thought?

Thought is our constant companion.

Thought is an elemental, energetic power that courses through our minds every moment of every day. Thought is always with us, creating our own unique, personalized experience of life.

We can't get away from this energy of thought, nor should we want to or need to. Thought is what enables us to navigate and communicate within the world in which we live.

The energy of thought flows through us constantly like a river.

Because of its flowing nature, we are continuously being delivered different thoughts at any given moment. Thoughts come into our system, flow through, and are replaced by new thoughts. This cycle of never-ending, ever-changing thought is happening *every moment of every day.*

We only have to sit quietly for a few moments and pay attention to what's happening in our head to see the truth of this.

There's a constant stream of thoughts within us-- coming and going, coming and going, coming and going...

Much like the waves of the ocean.

Coming and going. Coming and going...

Because of this, most of our thoughts go unnoticed.

We're continuously thinking, but a good portion is in the background. Consider it like an iceberg where we see the tip above water, but so much more of it lies beneath the surface.

This became clear to me very quickly during the closing "Savasana" sequence at the end of my first yoga class at the age of 50. Savasana is a sort of meditation where you lay on your mat and watch your thoughts come and go. Because I hadn't looked at my thoughts very closely before (other than a few "failed" attempts at meditation decades before), I was utterly shocked and amazed to see just how many thoughts were running through my head--*all at the same time!*

What I saw were layers upon layers upon layers of thought--at least 4 or 5 levels deep. Most seemed to be "thoughts about thoughts." As much as I tried to quiet them or make them go away, they weren't having any of it.

For the first couple of years of practicing yoga, I'd pay attention to my thoughts during Savasana, and wait for it to be over so I could go home and eat lunch. (My class was at noon, so one layer of thinking was almost always on the subject of what I might eat!)

What I later came to realize was that all those layers of thought I was witnessing on my yoga mat *were with me all the time*--whether I was aware of them or not. While their content was always changing, the fact that they were there, did not.

Thoughts upon thoughts upon thoughts in a constant swirl in the back of my mind.

Yet until, or unless, I was looking at them, I wasn't aware of their presence. More importantly, what I also didn't notice were *all the feelings* this constant stream of thoughts created in their wake.

You see, every thought comes with its own feeling attached to it. (I'll explain more about this later.) Because a good portion of my thoughts just so happened to be anxiety-laden, I felt anxious a lot of the time.

When I think about it now, it seems incredible that I was as functional in life as I was, given that I was walking around with a humongous head filled with anxious thoughts.

Yet so is the average person on the street-- including YOU!

Chapter 9: The Role of Thought in Anxiety

Our heads are filled with a constant stream of thoughts--many of which are not very nice, nor fun. While we all have our own unique "flavor" of thoughts based on our personal upbringing and worldview, from what I can tell, the negative ones tend to fall into common categories:

Anxious thoughts, sad thoughts, judgmental thoughts, angry thoughts, jealous thoughts, lack of self-esteem thoughts, grandiose thoughts, paranoid thoughts and many more.

Even so, our thinking is 100% personalized to us.

While some of us tend to have depressed thoughts, others may lean towards angry thoughts. Interestingly enough, depression and anger as well as most other category of negative thought, often stem from fearful thinking--otherwise known as anxiety.

Everyone has anxious or fearful or scared thinking.

Yet very often we think we're the only one.

Being afraid seems to be an evolutionary protection mechanism to keep us safe. Having a bit of internal fear back in the caveman days would certainly keep us on our toes and leery of predators.

Still today, there are times when it's important to be somewhat fearful. For instance, it's good to be wary of moving cars so that we don't walk out in front of them. And it's good to be cautious of hot stoves to avoid burning ourselves.

Yet in our modern world, a lot of our fears and anxiety are less than helpful--especially when they are our constant companions.

When anxious thoughts are always swirling around in the back of our heads (like they were for me most of my life), it's hard to function at our best. For some people, in certain circumstances, this can become debilitating and make it difficult to function at all.

In the pages that follow, we'll take a closer look at what anxiety is, where it comes from and the problems it causes. More importantly, we'll explore how anxiety can be viewed in a different light so that it no longer has the power to control our lives.

Chapter 10: The Nitty-Gritty of Anxiety

Where does anxiety come from?

Scary situations? Other people? Stuff that's happening outside of our control? Things we don't want to do?

Most of us believe that outside situations are what cause our anxiety, which certainly seems logical. We see a creepy-looking bug and we feel scared. As a result, it's easy to conclude that the scary bug *made us* feel scared, i.e., gave us a little hit of anxiety.

But not everyone is scared of bugs.

Some people might see the same bug and think it's cute. No anxiety there. So if it's the bug giving us anxiety, how come it doesn't give it to everyone? What if the bug was crawling on us, but we didn't notice it? Would we still be anxious?

And speaking of bugs, here's a quick, true story that further illustrates my point...

One day, while making one of my healthy lunches, I had taken the stem off of a vine-ripened tomato, set it aside on a napkin, and then forgot about it. After lunch while absent-mindedly cleaning up, I grabbed the napkin. Out of the corner of my eye, I saw what looked like a creepy spider. My heart rate went up; I gasped, and reflexively dropped the napkin. Within seconds, I realized what it really was, and my fear suddenly turned to amusement.

So what happened?

When I was thinking there was a spider on the napkin, my fight or flight response kicked in and the chemicals that go with it flooded my body. Once I saw that it was nothing harmful, my thoughts naturally changed and I calmed down. This clearly shows how it's not things outside of us (such as a spider or a mean person) that cause us fear, but our thoughts about those things.

This is the kind of real life example I want you to start noticing in your in your own life. They're happening all around you every day. In fact, before reading on, can you think of a situation, such as my "tomato stem spider," where you thought something was scary, only to find out it was really nothing at all? I hope you will try to think of one, as it will help you see the truth in what's coming next.

Outside things and circumstances can't cause anxiety.

Let's take public speaking for example. (If public speaking is a breeze for you, please substitute your fear of choice! Roller coasters? Blind dates? Your kids' health?)

A good portion of you reading this right now may be terrified of public speaking. You may have had to do it at some point--perhaps at school or for your job. And you may have been pretty scared. In fact, it's possible that just the thought of public speaking as you're reading this now has got your heart racing a little bit faster or your stomach feeling tied in knots.

Which is exactly my point.

Right now if you're feeling even the tiniest bit of anxiety when simply *reading about* public speaking, then it can't be the public speaking itself that causes anxiety.

Presumably you're not actually speaking in public right now. So how can it be the public speaking causing your anxiety? It can't. But because you're reading about speaking in public, your thoughts have gone there and may have turned sour.

Anxiety, as well as all of our feelings, comes to us directly and *only* through the power of thought in the moment.

Let's look at this a bit deeper.

All anxiety really is, is the uncomfortable physical feelings that are present within us, due to our conscious or unconscious thoughts.

Here's an example of how it works:

The power of thought that is constantly streaming through us comes into our heads and is filtered through everything that has ever happened to us, as well as what's been on our mind lately.

Let's say we have to give a presentation in a meeting at work for the big boss in a few days. Some of the thought energy flowing through our head may land and get stuck on the topic of that presentation.

It might be helpful here to picture the "thought flow" as a stream. (We'll call it the Thought Stream.)

Now let's imagine that individual thoughts are sticks gently floating within the Thought Stream. (We'll call them Thought Sticks.)

And let's picture the impending presentation as a large rock sticking up in the middle of the stream (we'll call it the Presentation Rock). It's there among many other rocks that represent situations (or even people) in your life. There may also be a Spouse Rock, a Mother Rock, a general Work Rock, etc.

As the Thought Sticks are floating down the Thought Stream, imagine one of them happens upon the large Presentation Rock and gets stuck there. When the Thought Stick is attached to and stuck on the Presentation Rock, it creates "Presentation Thoughts." And for those who have decided that presentations are scary, it turns the Presentation Thought into a "Scary Presentation Thought."

Remember, the thoughts (and Thought Sticks) themselves are neutral until we give them meaning. If a Thought Stick lands on a situational rock relating to something we like, for example, an Ice Cream Rock, it creates a "Yummy Ice Cream thought." But that same Ice Cream Rock with a Thought Stick attached could also create a "Guilty Ice Cream thought" if we're attempting to lose weight and believe we shouldn't be eating ice cream at the moment.

There is no one particular thought that any situation must always create.

Once attached to a situational rock, a Thought Stick may loosen up quickly, become free from its rock, float away downstream, and its resulting thought may be barely be noticed. Other times a Thought Stick may get deeply wedged into a situational rock and stay around for a while.

When this happens in our presentation example, for instance, Scary Presentation Thought now becomes SCARY PRESENTATION THOUGHT! Then it's all we can think about, and it seems to take up all the space in our head.

That's what stuck sticks (thoughts) do!

If it were only scary thoughts that got stuck, it might not be so bad. However, the thing with thoughts is that they also come with feelings attached.

So let's now imagine the Thought Sticks as having jagged edges or lots of sharp twigs sticking out of them. The twigs are the *feelings* that come with the thoughts. They poke at and into the rock while the stick is stuck--and it hurts.

Sad thought sticks come with sad twig feelings. Angry thought sticks come with mad twig feelings. Scary thought sticks come with anxious twig feelings.

We can imagine (and may very well have experienced) the anxious twig feelings that are attached to the SCARY PRESENTATION THOUGHTS.

Those feelings may manifest in any or all of these bodily sensations:

- Jitters
- Heart palpitations
- Stomach ache

- Flushness
- Tightness in the chest
- Sweating
- Shortness of breath
- Ticks or other repetitive movements
- Headaches
- High blood pressure

These feelings occur with our anxious thoughts in order to alert us to possible trouble.

In other words, our bodies are designed to produce certain chemicals during times of danger to keep us alert and safe, which is called the fight or flight response. This is what happens when we think there's something to be scared of. Those chemicals, in turn, cause specific feelings of anxiety within us, such as any of those in the bullet-point list above. (See the work of Hans Selye, if you're interested in more on this topic.)

Therefore, the feelings from anxiety are caused by the original scary thought and our body's reaction to it. Because the chemicals are triggered immediately in our bodies, we often don't even realize *we had a thought* about the situation. This tricks us into believing that it was the outside event that caused our anxious feelings. (E.g., believing that speaking in front of my boss and others at a meeting is the cause of me feeling scared/anxious.)

But again, that's only what it looks like when we don't know that our feelings are actually coming from the thoughts to which they are attached.

Often, what we're scared of are conditioned thoughts.

Something once happened--we got nervous or scared--so we associate that feeling with the event. As a protection mechanism, our bodies and minds want to remind us via anxious thinking and feelings to be cautious. So in the future when that, or a similar event occurs, we end up reacting the same way due to a conditioned thought/feeling response.

Unfortunately, thanks to our bodies and minds trying to be helpful, this can cause us to be scared of all sorts of things that don't present a danger to us NOW.

But here's the key thing to note, which we'll come back to later:

What is perceived as scary to one person isn't necessarily scary to another.

As previously mentioned, anxiety seems to be an evolutionary reaction to help us remain safe. Fear is a good way of keeping us out of physical harm by stopping us from doing unsafe things.

But in today's world, much of our anxiety is centered on preserving our ego rather than our physical body. A lot of what we're scared of now, are social things such as what others might think of us. There are probably evolutionary reasons for these types of thoughts, as well. For instance, the need to get along with our tribemates so we don't get ousted from the tribe. In times past, being kicked out of our tribe would have meant certain death.

But today, while it's still important to get along with our family, friends, colleagues and neighbors, worrying about what others think of us often ends up causing more problems than it alleviates.

Let's again take public speaking as an example.

It's not physically dangerous to give a presentation to a group. It's not going to kill us (even though it may feel that way!). But our thoughts (ego) tell us otherwise. "*Perhaps we will die from embarrassment*," we think. "*Perhaps everyone will believe we're stupid*," we think. "*Perhaps we won't be properly prepared*," we think.

Perhaps...perhaps...perhaps...

Any or all of those things might occur. Or they might not. We don't know.

But the anxiety stemming from our "future thinking" about what may or may not happen is often worse than the actual event itself.

Chapter 11: Anxiety Problems and Coping Strategies

Most of us come face-to-face with fear and anxiety every day on various levels. It affects us psychologically, socially and physically. Because anxiety is so pervasive, it can create a lot of problems and take quite a toll on our lives.

Psychological fears manifest in countless ways.

We can become afraid of anything--from truly scary situations, to everyday mundane ones such as meeting new people or even leaving the house. (Or getting your 6th grade schedule changed, or having a sick child, etc.)

Our fears can range in intensity from those we sort of know are silly but feel them anyway (fear of clowns anyone?), to ones where we can't cope and which impede us from living a full life--such as fear of flying, fear of doctors, etc.

From conversations I've had with people I've coached who seem to be "stuck," it's clear that social fears are extremely common, e.g., "*What will people think of me?*"

These fears, and the self-talk that comes with them, manifest throughout the day in various forms.

Most of us are so concerned with what we believe are the norms and rules of society and other people, we are often paralyzed in terms of how to live our own lives. (As an aside, it's my belief that everyone else is usually so consumed by their own fears and desires that, while they may judge us for a moment, they're usually back to thinking about themselves again fairly quickly!)

Unfortunately, our fears and anxieties are also the cause of many physical problems we encounter.

Living in a constant state of unconscious or conscious nervousness causes the fight or flight chemicals to be ever-present in our bodies. However, our bodies aren't designed to withstand this sort of onslaught. Prolonged exposure to these chemicals running through us can cause a host of physical symptoms. Many experts are starting to believe that even ailments such as heart disease and others often have their roots in the presence of these stress hormones.

Yet most of us don't realize this because the conditions *appear to* come from outside sources.

Because anxiety fills our heads with scary thoughts and causes so many psychological, social and physical problems, coping with it has become big business. When we're anxious, we want to feel better and we'll do just about anything to gain some peace of mind.

Which is where our coping strategies come in.

While some of us ignore our anxiety and plow through anyway, most of us consciously or unconsciously find things to do to keep our mind off of our bad feelings. This seems to provide us with the peace of mind we're seeking. Sadly, however, these coping strategies often turn into addictions such as drugs and alcohol, shopping, sex, needy relationships or work. (I used four out of those five!)

Even coping strategies that seem positive on the surface, such as prescription anxiety medications, or relaxation techniques such as meditation, exercise, music or deep breathing, don't get to the root of our anxiety issues. They can be very useful and helpful at calming down our thoughts and easing our nervousness when we are using them, but they're almost always temporary measures.

There is a better, easier, more permanent way to deal with and alleviate anxiety.

PART THREE:

UNCOVERING OUR INNER PEACE

Chapter 12: A Better Anxiety Solution

I've explained how anxiety is comprised of *the feelings* that come with thoughts. I also explained how thoughts, by their very nature and flow, come and go in and out of our heads.

While we don't have control over which thoughts pop in, our prior conditioning seems to cause certain ones to appear during specific situations.

But here's the missing piece of the conditioning puzzle:

Our prior conditioning itself is also made up of thought.

Just because something once seemed to make us anxious doesn't mean it will or has to continue to do so forevermore. When we see our prior conditioning for what it is, thoughts that have stuck with us over time, which we have now labeled as "beliefs," it can evaporate in an instant. What's left underneath this evaporated conditioning--is peace.

In fact, our natural state of mind is peacefulness.

Even in the midst of a whole lot of conditioned, anxious thoughts happening in our head, peace is right there below the surface. It's there for the taking, underneath our thinking.

Things crop up in life that seem to disturb our sense of peace, but when everything settles down, it's only peace that is left. What seems like a disturbance of the peace to us is actually *our thoughts* about whatever has cropped up--*not the situation itself.*

We know this to be true because not everyone is disturbed by the same situations. Again, I want you to seek out proof of this in your own life.

You might be scared to death of speaking in public, but others aren't. You might find riding on roller coasters to be fun and enjoyable, while others feel afraid. An extrovert probably loves chatting up strangers, while an introvert might find it a fate worse than death.

Therefore, the *anxiety itself* is simply a thought-created, made-up, belief system.

Here are some key things to note with regard to the feelings of anxiety and the thoughts that create them:

- **We are never forced to hold onto any particular thought or belief.** In our flowing river example, it's easy to see how the Thought Stick will eventually come loose from the Situational Rock. Sure, someone (us?) could come along and stand on the rock and hold onto that stick, but nobody is forcing us to do that with our thoughts in real life. We can *let them be* and they will eventually get loose, or we can simply let go of them. In fact, at some point, we always do. This, in turn, allows our natural flowing peaceful state to resurface.

- **There are no rules that say, "When this happens I have to be anxious."** While our conditioning, prior circumstances and very often society itself tries to make us believe there are such rules, there aren't. When we see a spider, there is no rule that says we have to be scared. It's the same when we have to speak in public, meet new people or fly in an airplane. Just because we've always been nervous in these situations in the past, doesn't mean it's a non-negotiable rule of life. Beliefs are not facts or rules. They are just thoughts that we keep thinking.

- **All thoughts come and go within our mind.** If we can remember this when we start to feel anxious, we can learn to be okay even in the midst of our anxiety. It is often the feeling that our anxious thoughts will never go away that creates fear on top of existing fears. Having a sense that the anxious thoughts are never permanent, and that peace is just a thought away, can sometimes ease our minds.

- **We don't even notice or "grab onto" most of our thoughts (anxious or otherwise)-- they simply float downstream.** This is helpful to know, because it reminds us that there are plenty of thoughts we don't pay attention to. They come and go, come and go, come and go. It's only when we hold onto thoughts that we become aware of them and their associated feelings. Some people grab onto their anxious ones more often, while others may gravitate to their angry or depressed thoughts.

- **Often, we don't even notice when we're anxious because we're so used to it that it seems normal.** This is because many (if not most) of our anxious thoughts are with us on an unconscious level. In other words, we *feel* the anxiety in some physical manner, but we aren't aware of the thoughts that have created it. So, just as I did for most of my life, we end up walking around in a constant state of anxiety, and assume that's simply how it's supposed to be.

But living with continuous feelings of anxiety does NOT have to be the norm.

As hard as it is to believe when we're so used to living with anxiety (or other stressful feelings)-- peacefulness is our default state of mind. In fact, it's our birthright and who we are at our core.

If not for the thoughts that create our bad feelings, there could be *only peace*. Calmness and, dare I say, even happiness, lie underneath our thinking. If we could stop thinking (which we can't), we'd see anxiety very clearly for what it is--stuck thoughts that trigger chemicals in our bodies, which create bad feelings. Full stop.

This knowing of what and where anxious feelings come from can sometimes bring us relief. If nothing else, it helps us to not pile more anxious thinking on top of the existing anxious thoughts. Understanding that our thoughts come and go, and that our anxious ones won't and can't stay forever, helps us move through the feelings with a little more grace.

But make no mistake about this--it is not about trying to *change your thoughts*.

That can only take you so far.

Remember this as you read on, because it's likely that your next question will be related to how to change your thoughts. That's *not at all* what I'm talking about, nor trying to convey.

Chapter 13: Remembering Your Natural State

The bottom line is that our innate, natural state of mind is peacefulness--not anxiousness.

Wellbeing always resides underneath any and all of our perceived fears. When we start to know this, our symptoms of anxiety begin to lose their hold on us and--in some cases--disappear altogether.

There's so much hope in this, not only for those who suffer from extreme anxiety, but for the average person on the street who's stressed out, burned out, depressed, fearful, lonely and what have you. So much hope for me, and so much hope for you.

Because let's face it, everyone feels (at least) a little bit crazy on the inside.

This is fairly evident when we lose it over the tiniest of things. Our day didn't go as planned. Our co-worker did that thing she always does that pisses us off. Our spouse seems to be ignoring us. Our kids are being rude. Someone in the supermarket gave us a disapproving look.

And on and on it goes.

We don't have to look too far to find something that seems to upset our peace.

And yet. And yet. And yet...

Our peace really can't be upset by those things happening in the outside world.

There's mental wellbeing--otherwise known as "peace"--inside of all of us. In our anxious, crazy, stressed out world it may not feel that way much of the time. But it's really true.

Think of our mind like a snow globe. When anxiety hits us, it gets all shaken up.

The snow in the globe is like our anxious thoughts-- all stirred up and kinda crazy. But at some point when we stop shaking it and let it be, just like the snow in the globe, our fearful thoughts settle down.

You can see this for yourself when something bad happens and your anxious thoughts/feelings kick into high gear. When you're in the middle of a nasty anxiety attack, it feels as if it's the worst thing ever and it's never going to stop. Yet it always does. At some point, the events that looked so bad have a different feel to them because our thoughts have changed. We get used to whatever situation we find ourselves having to deal with and it becomes our new "normal."

An example of this for me was when I was helping out a close family member who was suddenly diagnosed with cancer. The original prognosis was bleak. With that as a baseline, when biopsy results came back that it was a more treatable type of cancer, suddenly it was good news--despite the fact that it was still cancer. Had I heard the biopsy results first (without having lived some days with the bleak prognosis on my mind), I probably would not have seen it as good news. My previous "normal" was that any news about cancer was bad, bad and more bad.

To me, this incident clearly illustrated how it wasn't the outside situation causing my feelings, but my thoughts about it. If it were the situation, I would feel the same about any cancer diagnosis, regardless of the prognosis.

The thought storm *always* settles down once we let it.

What gets us into trouble is when we believe our thought storm is something *we need* to take action on. Just like we're increasing our chances of having an accident if we take a drive in the middle of a blizzard, it's the same with our thought storms. While we're in the midst of them, it feels as if we need to do something to rectify the situation. But because the only thing happening is that we're having anxious thoughts, all we really need to do is let them settle. The more we can do that, the less likely our anxiety will grow out of proportion.

How can we settle our anxious mind when scary stuff is seemingly happening all around us?

Well, how do you settle a snow globe?

You can try all sorts of ways of moving it around, but that's not going to work. It's simply a matter of putting it down and letting it settle all by itself. In other words, *letting it be*.

And it's the same with our minds.

If we can have the fortitude to not pile anxious thoughts on top of anxious thoughts and simply wait for our minds to settle--*as they have done every single time before*--we'll calm down a lot faster.

Once we understand that thoughts create our anxious feelings and that they will pass on their own, it's easier to simply let them be. There will no longer be a need to try and change them or somehow force them to go away.

We can just notice the fact that we're having an anxious moment and move on.

Chapter 14: Becoming Aware

If you're starting to grasp where anxiety stems from, you may be thinking, "Okay, I get that it's my thoughts that are creating my feelings of anxiety...so how do I change them?"

If so, you're missing my key point. (Don't feel bad, this is a new way of seeing things and most people wonder about this at first!) While it may sound similar to positive thinking, cognitive behavioral therapy (CBT), or other self-help concepts you may have learned in the past, it's not the same.

This has nothing to do with changing our thoughts. Nor is it about purposely trying NOT to think anxious thoughts.

Try to NOT think of a purple elephant and see how well that works.

Instead, when we see our anxiety at the deepest level for what it is--thought energy in the moment--and when we KNOW within the core of our being that *underneath all thought lies peace*, then we can simply let it be. At which point, the anxious thoughts (and the feelings that come with them) often start to fall away ALL BY THEMSELVES!

How do we see our anxious thoughts for what they are?

First, we have to become aware of our thoughts. For many of us, this means we have to become aware *that we are even thinking in the first place.* While most of us have some slight awareness of our thoughts, especially when they're loud or mean, most of us don't recognize *just how much* is going on in our heads at any time.

When we're not aware of our thoughts, we essentially live our lives as "robots" and are at the whim of whatever habitual ones happen to come to mind at any moment. Perhaps more problematic, it also means that we're at the mercy of all the feelings attached to those thoughts.

So we are literally being pushed and pulled and dragged along through life, thinking and doing and feeling crazy things, simply because of what randomly pops into our heads!

Is that any way to live?

No wonder we feel stressed and anxious most of the time.

In order to be free from anxiety's grip and to feel better overall, we've got to pay attention to what's going on inside of us. Thankfully, it's easier than you may think.

Certainly meditation can be helpful and is a good way to begin to see just how much thought is swirling around inside. I highly recommend trying it as you embark on your quest to become more aware of your thoughts. Please note that meditation, in the way I'm talking about it, doesn't mean you have to try to *quiet your mind*. You're likely to give up quickly if that's your goal.

All we're going for here is for you to become more aware of your thoughts by simply watching/noticing them.

While meditation isn't required to get a feel for how many thoughts are swirling around in your head, often sitting quietly for 10-20 minutes per day is an easy way to start to see it all in action. Once you've done this even just a few times, you'll have a better sense of the volume of thoughts flowing through you. You'll also learn that it is possible to observe some thoughts as they're happening. However, I realize that meditation is off-putting to some, so if you can't seem to do it, or it makes you too uncomfortable, or you just don't want to take the time--that's okay. The idea is to create awareness of your thoughts, not torture you!

What I found the most helpful was simply observing my thoughts *throughout my regular day*.

Here's why that's important:

Because we generally live our lives without ever noticing our thoughts, most of the time we act unconsciously--allowing our reactive habits and behaviors to take over.

Where anxiety is concerned, this is a recipe for disaster. We have an anxious thought--and poof--we feel anxious. Because the feeling comes with the thought, it seems as if we have no choice in the matter.

Which is where observing our thoughts comes in.

As I started to observe my thoughts throughout my day, I noticed quickly just how many thoughts I was having that I hadn't been aware of. It was pretty crazy.

Or rather, *I seemed* very crazy!

I had a constant stream of chatter and comments about *everything* going on around me at any given moment. I also noticed thoughts about the past and thoughts concerning what might happen in the future. All of these were coming at me at once! If nothing else, observing my thoughts gave me a deeper appreciation of how our amazing mind is capable of having thoughts of past, present and future--simultaneously.

The cool part is what happened next.

Chapter 15: Clear Skies Ahead

I have no idea how long it took--hours, days, weeks or months--but at some point during my observations, the chatter in my head calmed down. It was as if the thoughts couldn't exist while being watched. (I liken it to shining a light on cockroaches.) Now don't get me wrong, I still had plenty of thoughts, but there weren't as many dimensions to them.

I found that I was having fewer thoughts *about the thoughts*, if that makes sense. And without as many thoughts, there was suddenly more space in my head.

This newly created "empty space" enabled my underlying sense of peace to bubble up to the surface. Or more accurately, the space itself--*was* peace.

There were times, like when on my yoga mat, that it felt and looked as if the clouds in my mind had parted and there was nothing but clear blue sky all around. The sense of peace was like none I had experienced before, and it was kind of scary because it felt so unusual. (Paradoxically, my being scared disturbed my peace and brought the thoughts back again!)

But the more I kept observing and becoming aware of my thoughts, the more I got used to the clear blue sky mind I was experiencing.

Eventually, this quiet, more peaceful space became my norm.

These days, I don't consciously observe my thoughts, yet it continues to happen naturally through general awareness. It's a lot easier now because there are fewer thoughts to observe. I've gotten used to having a clearer mind, so I can't help but notice when I get caught up in a major thought storm. Rather than my default, vast blue sky, it's like a mega thunderstorm complete with dark clouds, lightning and tons of booming thunder!

When my natural state of peace is pushed down below the surface, I can't distinguish one thought from another. But I do notice the awful feelings that come along for the ride. As you can imagine--just like with the outside weather--I much prefer the clear, sunny days in my head, and the calm, easy feelings in my body.

Through my awareness, I'm no longer a victim of my thoughts.

Because they can't hide from me and I know the feelings associated with them, I notice my anxious thoughts more quickly. This, in turn, helps me recognize them for what they are--meaningless thought energy. Once they're identified as such, it's a lot easier for me to not attach my own meaning to them.

Basically, I let them be.

For it's the meaning we attach to our thoughts that causes them to stick around.

Without meaning, none of our thoughts have any power on their own. They are just that flowing energy amidst our peaceful stream that comes and goes.

Knowing this helps me be less inclined to react or hold on to the "crazy" ones--usually felt as anxiety.

Until I started observing my thoughts, however, I had no idea how much anxiety was coursing through my brain All. Day. Long. No idea at all. I only noticed it under the scariest circumstances, or when the physical sensations became too much to bear.

When I think about it now, it's hard to imagine how I managed to be a functional and successful person, given how cluttered my mind was with anxious thoughts.

Without awareness, there was nothing I could do but allow anxiety to run my life.

Striving to feel better (without consciously realizing it) was my main goal in life. Whatever means I could find to soothe myself was the order of the day. This is where alcohol, my computer, my best friends, my husband, my kids and my other addictive "substances" came into play.

The good news is:

By being aware of my feelings and shining a constant light on my thoughts, i.e., bringing them into my conscious awareness through observation, they were magically transmuted into nothingness.

Which is the ultimate freedom.

When our anxious thoughts don't feel quite as uncomfortable to us, we have less (or no) need for our old soothing addictive behaviors. Especially when we also know that our peaceful state is there for the taking--underneath the anxious thoughts.

Once we recognize the feeling of innate peacefulness bubbling up to the surface, we begin to experience it more often. Which is when our lives are transformed forever!

If there's one practice or "doing" that I would prescribe to you, it's to start observing your thoughts. I can't guarantee you'll have the same results I did, but it certainly can't hurt. The benefits for me throughout my transformational journey have been nothing short of amazing. Being more consciously aware has taught me more about life than anything else I've heard or read.

Awareness is the key to a clearer mind, feeling better, freedom from addictions and a whole new world of possibilities!

Chapter 16: Being Less Scared of Being Scared

If I'm giving the impression that I never feel anxious anymore, I apologize--because I still do.

However, understanding that those feelings are caused by anxious thoughts, which have no power on their own, means it doesn't usually bother me the way it used to. Even when it does, I'm able to cope without the need for outside sources such as alcohol, work, or needy relationships.

In truth, it's not about coping at all. There is nothing I have to do about my anxious feelings. (Not that I could even if I tried.)

Here's how it often goes down for me...

Because I'm aware of my feelings, I'll sometimes notice out of nowhere that I'm suddenly experiencing the early signs of anxiety. I may become aware of my heart racing and/or my head or stomach beginning to hurt, yet I have no conscious idea of why.

When I first started noticing this, in order to prove to myself that it was, in fact, thoughts creating my anxious feelings, I decided to trace back what the causative thoughts were. In doing this interesting exercise, I was able to find the one (or more) thoughts that seemed to come from nowhere to cause my nervousness.

For me, it was usually little worries that popped up, like wondering how my kids were doing or thinking about some project on which I had been procrastinating.

The more I traced back my anxious feelings, the clearer it was that 100% of the time they were associated with anxious thoughts.

Once I knew this for certain, I no longer had the need to keep tracing back my anxious feelings to thoughts; I had the proof I needed to be certain how the system worked. I could simply notice when I was feeling anxious and say to myself, *"Hmm...I guess I'm having an anxious thought again!"* In most cases, this was enough for the feeling to pass quickly, and peace to return.

These days, I no longer even bother to say anything to myself. I might still notice the early signs of anxiety, but because I know it will pass soon enough on its own, I generally don't give it any attention.

I implore you to seek your own evidence and try this out the next time you feel any bit of anxiety coming on. It's important for you to prove to yourself that it is, in fact, thoughts that produce the feelings you're having. Do this as often as it takes for you to have no doubt that this is how your system works.

Knowing the truth of the "Thought - Feeling Connection" is the key for you to start feeling better.

Once you're convinced, you'll be better equipped to simply dismiss or let your thoughts be, rather than continuing to chase them down. This will help you be less scared of being scared; because it's only when we feel the anxiety push our peace below the surface and get frightened by it, that it causes problems.

Over time, as your belief turns to Knowing and you have more than just an intellectual understanding of the thought-feeling connection, situations you previously thought *caused* your anxiety simply won't anymore. After all, when you believed the opposite-- that the situation was the cause of your anxious feelings--you were powerless. But with your new understanding, even when you still experience some anxiety, it becomes easier to give the emotion less attention. Especially when you also know that beneath the surface of the bad feelings, peacefulness awaits!

Of course, this sounds well and good when we're feeling fine, or when we have just a little bit of nervousness. And I'm not going to lie--it's easy to forget when we're in the middle of a really bad anxiety attack. When something is desperately awry (or we believe that it is), even when we Know it has to be coming from our own thinking, it's still going to feel like the outside circumstances are causing our reaction.

This is why it's so important to be vigilantly aware of what's going on inside of us.

Chapter 17: Next Steps

Here are six steps you can take over the next few days, weeks or months to help this information sink in. Ideally, it will keep you more aware and prove that it really and truly is *your thoughts* that are creating your anxious feelings on top of your natural, peaceful state.

1. **Notice when you feel anxious.** This may be easier said than done if you live in a general state of anxiety. But if you've been starting to observe your thoughts and pay attention to how you feel at any given time during the day, you'll become more aware of when you're anxious and when you're not. (It helps to also notice how you feel when you're peaceful.)

2. **When you do feel anxious, see if you can trace back the thought or thoughts that caused the feeling.** Do this by simply observing the thoughts going through your head at the time. Again, it's all about becoming more aware and paying attention to your thoughts and feelings.

3. **Decide if there is a valid (safety) reason to which you need to pay attention.** Once you trace back the thought that has disturbed your peace, you should have some idea of what it's about. Obviously, if there's an intruder in your home or some other immediate problem, you'll want to take care of it. Those are the type of valid thoughts worth listening to. However, don't trick yourself into believing invalid ones to be valid. Most of them aren't!

4. **Determine if the scary thoughts have no immediate implications.** Most likely you'll find that what triggered your anxiety-laden feelings are just some random thoughts that popped into your head. They may be based on something you were doing, reading, watching, or seeing--or not. The trigger doesn't matter.

5. **Notice if anxious feelings happened because of your past conditioning to those types of thoughts**. It's highly likely that whatever thoughts disturbed your peace occurred due to some past associations with that particular kind of thought. For instance, if in the past when your spouse came home in a bad mood you ended up arguing, the thought of him or her coming home in that state could create the association with arguing.

6. **Decide if being scared NOW serves any real purpose.** In the case of thinking about something that may (or may not) happen in the future such as your partner's state of mind, or if your kid is safe, there's really no purpose or reason to think about it, ruminate on it, wonder about it, worry about it or feel anxious about it *right now*. When you start to see that nothing is actually happening to you at this moment other than you having some random thoughts, it's easier to let them be and allow them to pass through you.

At first, the above steps may not be easy for you, especially if you're already in an anxious state. This is because when we're in a full-blown anxiety attack (or even a minor one) it generally consists of many thoughts coming at us all at once. A lot of them will be unconscious and difficult to notice. Even when we're used to observing our minds and looking at our thoughts, it isn't always possible in the midst of one of these full-on attacks.

But that's okay.

We can still identify the anxious feelings that have covered over our peaceful state--and know that they will pass.

What may be helpful when you can't distinguish one thought from another is to reflect on the situation after the fact.

- Can you think of a time in recent memory (earlier today, yesterday, this week) where you remember feeling anxious?

- What were the thoughts associated with the feelings?

- Was there a good reason to hold onto those thoughts?

- Or were they just a conditioned response based on past experiences or learning?

Once you have an "aha" moment and truly get that it's our thoughts creating our feelings in life, the next important element is to grasp that our natural state of being is peace and goodness and happiness. (Really!)

Chapter 18: Insights--The Key to True Understanding

The real power in this knowledge comes when you have a deep insight into the nature of how it works. An intellectual understanding is certainly helpful, but it's deep insights that magically cause spontaneous change.

If you're not familiar with insights, they are simply "Aha" or "Eureka" moments. If you have been reading this book with your skepticism on hold and you were a little lucky, you may have even had one or more insights already. (That's been my aim for you.)

An insight is when you suddenly see something at a deep level that you never saw before.

Like with an optical illusion or those 3D "Magic Eye" pictures. You look and look and look, then in a flash, you simply see it.

It's the same with insights. You may have heard something a million times before, but now it makes sense in a new way--at a deeper level. It suddenly becomes more than just an intellectual understanding.

It becomes a Knowing.

When that happens, you'll never be able to look at things the old way. In other words, once you know the truth, e.g., that the spider is actually a tomato stem, you can't go back to seeing it as a spider--ever again.

My first insight into this new way of understanding the world was that "thoughts create our feelings." I heard many of my mentors say it numerous times, but I didn't understand what it really meant--*until I did*!

For me, it took hearing it at a time when I had a relatable experience the night before.

Because insight into the thought-feeling connection is so critical to this book having any effect on you, I'll tell you how it went down for me. Perhaps you'll be able to relate to something similar in your own life...

One night, when the dinner I was cooking was ready, I looked over at my husband and asked if he was ready to eat. He didn't respond, so I assumed he didn't hear me and asked again. After a few seconds he said, "Okay."

However, *in my mind,* he didn't say it in a way that sounded like he really was ready to eat. I felt it was more like how a kid might say it if you asked if they were ready to leave the playground when they really weren't but knew they had to. I even replied back (although I'm not sure if he heard me) "*that doesn't sound very convincing.*"

At any rate, we ate dinner, but it wasn't the most pleasant experience for me. My thoughts kept going back to his "*Okay*" (one word mind you!). I couldn't stop wondering what it was all about.

"Did he not like my cooking? Was he sick of eating at home?" We used to go out most nights, but I had been making an effort to cook more. "Was he not hungry? Was he just not ready to stop scrolling through Facebook?"

I suppose I could have just asked, but I didn't.

He seemed to enjoy the food, helped clean up and went back to his computer. Meanwhile, I was still in my head angry and/or hurt--because he said, "Okay"!

A bit later, he was on his way out for the night and left without saying goodbye. So now, I was doubly mad. In my head was, "Why didn't he say goodbye? Is he mad at me? Does he think I'm mad at him? Doesn't he know I hate it when he doesn't say goodbye? Did he want me to come with him, but knew I wouldn't?"

All this thinking in my head without him even saying another word!

So basically, I got myself in a tizzy through my thoughts.

In fact, my thinking about it ruined most of my night. Those thoughts all evening long were stressing me out. I could feel the tension in my jaw (even just thinking about it as I'm writing this is causing a little tension), and I'm pretty sure my blood pressure was some points higher than usual.

Looking at this incident within the new paradigm, it's easy for me to see that my thoughts were making me unhappy. But if you haven't yet had the insight that our thoughts create the way we feel, you're probably thinking, "*No, it was your husband making you feel unhappy*"!

But that's not true.

Sure, my unhappy thoughts may have been triggered by the situation at hand, but he didn't (nor can he) make me unhappy himself. *Only my thoughts can do that.* And whether or not he knew I was unhappy, or whether or not he purposely did anything to make me unhappy, is irrelevant.

It's only my thoughts that can make me unhappy. Full stop.

Here's the interesting part that further proves the point. For a while I was holding onto my mad feelings by saying things to myself like, "*When he comes home I'm not going to even talk to him. That'll teach him! He needs to know how unhappy he's making me.*"

But eventually, I got tired of feeling unhappy.

And I also logically knew that being a jerk to him when he came home would likely only cause more unhappiness--probably for both of us. Instead, I decided to just be normal (what a concept!). Even without having imbued the idea that it was my thoughts causing my upset, I did intellectually understand that the saying of one word is not really a battle worth fighting.

I ended up taking my mind off of the whole thing (not purposely) by doing what I normally would have done that evening. When he came home it was fairly late. And while I could have been asleep, or pretending to be, I decided to interact with him. He told me about his night and all was back to normal.

What I didn't realize at the time, or perhaps I did unconsciously, was all that had happened was *my thoughts had changed.* Doing other things rather than dwelling on my anger seemed to enable my thoughts to run their course.

The Thought Stick was no longer stuck to the Situational Rock and was allowed to float freely downstream.

Recalling that incident while at the same time hearing one of my mentors say in a video that *thoughts create our feelings* spurred my "aha moment." The fact that I had just had an experience in alignment with what I was learning gave me something to relate to. And an insight suddenly occurred--BOOM!

- Can you think of a situation where you created a story in your head about something that was happening in your life? (Note that it probably didn't seem like a "story" at the time.) Try to be as honest as you can with yourself as you ponder this.

- Can you see how it's *always* thought that causes our feelings and not the other way around?

Can you imagine how understanding this at a deeper level could have a profound effect on your anxiety and your life in general?

Chapter 19: When Old Behaviors Simply Drop Away

Now that you know what an insight is, and perhaps have even had one or more while reading this book, I'll let you in on the real power of this Understanding. While knowing about thoughts and feelings and everything else I've been talking about is super helpful...

Insights have a power of their own that goes well beyond a helpful knowing.

Some insights are seen and felt at such a deep level that they have a sort of special power behind or within them. They have an almost magical quality that can erase or delete years and even decades of habits and psychological conditioning.

These special insights automatically and effortlessly change our life.

In other words, with some insights, suddenly (or gradually), those things we used to do, or those feelings we used to have--simply disappear.

I was lucky enough to have been gifted with one of these very magical insights. Here's how it happened...

As has been shown in this book, I always knew I had an addictive personality. From friendships, to my husband, to my computer, to my kids, to alcohol--I immersed myself in whatever--until the next thing came along. As noted, it wasn't all bad as this propelled me into my successful career, and I raised three great children, etc.

But in other cases, my obsessions were less than helpful.

For instance, I cringe when I think about the numerous friendships I killed by being too clingy-- starting back in first grade and continuing throughout my adult life. I see now that in each relationship I was always looking towards the other to make me happy; which they did--until they didn't. And it played out in my family life, as well as with my drinking alcohol as a means of trying to feel better.

The problem with alcohol and the other addictions was that they were temporary solutions. They made me feel good while they lasted, but they were coming from outside of me so they eventually wore off. As I started to learn how life really worked, and that happiness and peace were already inside of me (and who I am at my core), I also started to see the reasons for my addictive behaviors.

It all came to a head when I had a "life flashing before my eyes" moment.

Apparently, you can have them even when you're not about to die!

All at once in a quick flash as I was taking a shower, I got a download from the Universe that showed me my long string of addictions beginning from when I was a little kid until the present moment. I saw clearly how they were all my attempt to seek happiness outside of myself.

In other words, I was looking for peace in all the wrong places. I realized in that flash that my "outside-in" way of thinking had caused each and every addiction.

In that moment of realization, I insightfully saw that what I was seeking all along, was who I already was deep inside.

I *knew* as clear as day how my addictions were merely my way of attempting to change my thoughts to help me feel good. I hadn't previously understood that good feelings were *always only a thought away*--with or without my obsessions.

Prior to this realization, my mind (like most) was constantly reminding me of all the bad things that have happened or could happen--even if I wasn't consciously aware of it. It wasn't until I had this major insight that I was able to recognize how all of my obsessions and addictions throughout my life were an attempt to keep my thoughts focused elsewhere. As long as I was obsessed with something or someone, I didn't hear (as much) those insecure voices in my head.

Now, just from my Knowing that all along it was my thoughts that had been creating my feelings, and that at any time those thoughts could (and do) change, *I no longer needed my old obsessive addictive catalysts to change them for me.*

From that moment on, I gained a new level of clarity.

That new state of mind led to fewer anxious thoughts sneaking in and grabbing me without warning.

I've gotten to see this play out in so many ways.

One of the first things I noticed was that I no longer needed to have music playing in the background all the time. I had no idea that I was unconsciously using a constant stream of music as a method of distracting myself from anxious thoughts. On the other hand, I pat myself on the back for managing to come up with that harmless coping strategy!

More importantly, this knowledge has also played out in a big way regarding alcohol.

I used to feel that if I was going to have any drinks at all, I wanted to at least get some sort of buzz out of it (after all, why waste the calories!). Now I have the exact opposite feeling. I still drink alcohol, but I'm not the least bit interested in getting buzzed. In fact, if I drink too fast and start to feel a buzz, I am uncomfortable.

It's as if I'm taking my nice calm mind and screwing it up. I can absolutely take or leave alcohol right now, which you would never have heard me say at other times in my life. I simply don't need it like I used to.

Seeing my past behaviors and relationships in this new light is fascinating.

I'm impressed with our mind's ability to find all sorts of coping mechanisms to deal with anxiety and the ups and downs of life. I think I intuitively knew all along that our default setting is peace and happiness, and that's what got me through the bad times. But I sure wish I hadn't spent so long looking in the wrong direction for it!
It's time for you to start looking in the right direction.

I hope this book has given you enough information to explore where your anxiety *really* comes from. And I hope that once you've collected enough evidence, you will gain some amazing insights into your own life that will transform it forever!

But be kind to yourself. Even after you've had insights, it's easy to forget and slip back into believing that other people and situations are causing you grief. Believe me, this still happens to me every day.

No matter how many insights we have, we're still human. And for whatever reason, we quite innocently believe the world and the other humans in it can cause us pain and anxiety. When you slip back into old ways of thinking, try not to beat yourself up over it. That just increases your bad feelings.

The best thing you can do for yourself is to keep seeking evidence of the thought-feeling connection. And, as my original mentor, Michael Neill always says, "Continue to stay in the conversation."

PART FOUR:

WHERE TO GO FROM HERE

A whole new way of seeing the world doesn't often come from reading one book for a few hours. While all the information you need to start to see through your anxiety and begin to feel better is provided in this book (and I encourage you to read it multiple times), you should also investigate further.

First, please feel free to reach out to me. I'm very accessible and am always happy to answer any questions you may have about the book, anxiety, or anything else on your mind. You can contact me by email at:
anxietybook@whatdidyoudowithjill.com.

Also, please sign up for my free newsletter and read my blog posts over at:
WhatDidYouDoWithJill.com

Plus, be sure to join the free Facebook Group I've created for readers of this book. You'll find it here:
https://www.facebook.com/groups/ anxietyillusion/

But don't stop there.

Although I haven't specifically talked about what "The Three Principles" are, most of what's written in this book is based on that particular "understanding."

There are a growing number of those, who like me, have seen through the illusion of an outside-in world. Many have written books and articles, and created videos on the "Thought-Feeling" connection.

My first insight came when watching a video of Jenny and Rudi Kennard, as I heard a different perspective from what I had heard from Michael Neill. Therefore, I encourage you to also learn from others. Sometimes when you hear a slightly different take on the same message, it can trigger your own "aha moment."

The resources below are a very small sampling of some of my favorites, which should be enough to get you started.

Michael Neill: Michael is a best-selling author and coach who has brought so many people (including me) to this new understanding of life via his radio show, his newsletter, his programs, his coaching and his books. You can find him and all that he does at **MichaelNeill.org**. I will be forever grateful for stumbling across him originally through his online radio program with HayHouse.

Dr. Amy Johnson: Amy is a psychologist, coach and author who has an awesome weekly free newsletter, and a couple of great books on the same understanding I've written about here. She often writes about habits and addictions, as well as eating disorders. You can find out more about her and her work at **DrAmyJohnson.com**. She's recently started an online school called, "**The Little School of Big Change**" which I highly recommend as a great next step in learning more about the inside-out nature of life.

Sydney Banks: Syd was the original "founder" of the Three Principles understanding in that he had an enlightenment experience, and shared what he saw and learned with others. Sadly, there are not a whole lot of his videos and audios publicly available on YouTube. You can find a few on the Three Principles Movies website, and others can be found at the **3PGC.org** website. In addition, he wrote many books before his death in 2009, which you can learn about at **SydneyBanks.org** and purchase from Amazon. Please note that much of Syd's work has a more spiritual tone than that of others, especially his older work. I was glad to have already learned a bit about the Three Principles before finding Syd's stuff as I probably wouldn't have been ready for it at the beginning of my journey. These days, however, one of my favorite books is Syd's ultra-spiritual book called The Missing Link.

Three Principles Movies: If you prefer watching and listening over reading, this site created by Rudi Kennard and Jenny Anderson contains a treasure trove of Three Principles videos. It's a great place to learn more about what the three principles actually are, as well as watch interviews and workshops. You'll find it all at **ThreePrinciplesMovies.com**.

Mary Schiller: Mary discovered this understanding around the same time as I did, and has since written several books on this topic. Her story of the PTSD she had suffered from for decades--simply disappearing--is fascinating and highly compelling. You can learn more about her at **MarySchiller.com.**

The 3 Principles Essential Resources Guide: For even more resources, Dr. Anne Curtis has put together an up-to-date resource guide. It can be downloaded from her **3 Principles Resources Facebook Group**.

About the Author

For over 50 years, while having a happy family life and successful career as a pioneer in the website marketing industry, Jill Whalen's internal life was filled with anxiety. That changed when she discovered that it was her thoughts creating her anxious feelings rather than other people and situations. With a few insightful "aha moments," her anxiety no longer had the same hold on her as it once did.

She has spent the last four years documenting her transformation in her blog, "What Did You Do With Jill?" and helping others who are seeking change within their lives.

Jill loves to point people in the direction of uncovering their natural well-being and happiness so that they can operate from a clearer state of mind. She provides one-on-one mentoring to individuals, coaches, small business owners, leaders, groups and organizations. She also teaches workshops and seminars on topics such as relationships, stress, anxiety, and effortless success through passion power.

Jill is a mentor within the "Primal Happiness Thrive Community" and a faculty member of "Three Principles Supermind."

Stay abreast of Jill's latest musings and offerings by subscribing to her newsletter at WhatDidYouDoWithJill.com.